ESSENTIAL MANAGERS

Managing People

PHILLIP L. HUNSAKER & JOHANNA S. HUNSAKER

D0967089

London, New York, Melbourne,
Munich, and Delhi

Senior Editor Peter Jones
Editor Daniel Mills
US Editor Margaret Parrish
Senior Art Editor Helen Spencer
Production Editor Ben Marcus
Production Controller Hema Gohil
Executive Managing Editor Adèle Hayward
Managing Art Editor Kat Mead
Art Director Peter Luff
Publisher Stephanie Jackson

Produced for Dorling Kindersley Limited by

cobaltid

The Stables, Wood Farm, Deopham Road,
Attleborough, Norfolk NR17 1AJ
www.cobaltid.co.uk

Editors Kati Dye, Maddy King,
Marek Walisiewicz
Designers Paul Reid, Lloyd Tilbury

First American Edition, 2009

Published in the United States by DK Publishing
375 Hudson Street, New York, New York 10014

10 11 12   10 9 8 7 6 5 4 3 2

ND133—June 2009

Copyright © 2009 Dorling Kindersley Limited
All rights reserved

Without limiting the rights under copyright reserved
above, no part of this publication may be reproduced, stored
in or introduced into a retrieval system, or transmitted, in any
form, or by any means (electronic, mechanical, photocopying,
recording, or otherwise), without the prior written permission of
both the copyright owner and the above publisher of this book.

Published in Great Britain by
Dorling Kindersley Limited.

A catalog record for this book is available from
the Library of Congress.

ISBN 978-0-7566-4286-0

DK books are available at special discounts
when purchased in bulk for sales promotions,
premiums, fund-raising, or educational use.
For details, contact: DK Publishing Special Markets,
375 Hudson Street, New York, New York 10014 or
SpecialSales@dk.com.

Color reproduction by Colorscan, Singapore
Printed and bound in China by Starlite Development

Discover more at **www.dk.com**

Contents

CHAPTER 3

Managing a team

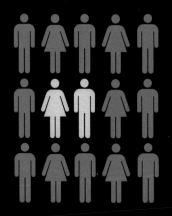

CHAPTER 4

Leading others

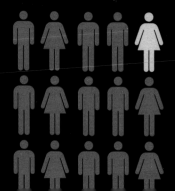

Introduction

Managing other people is perhaps the most challenging task facing any manager. It is a dynamic process that is always evolving to accommodate changes in the diverse and complex workplace. *Managing People* provides the understanding and skills that will help you to develop and manage effective and high-performing teams of satisfied and productive individuals.

Being an effective manager of people starts with self-awareness and self-management. Interpersonal skills are extremely important, in both one-on-one and team situations, as you need to be able to influence others to accomplish their own and the organization's goals. Creating high-performing teams is crucial for any manager today and requires the abilities to set goals, plan and design work, delegate tasks, motivate followers, appraise performance, and solve problems.

As a leader of your team, you need to invest considerable time in helping others to improve their performance and develop their careers. Successful mentoring can contribute to fulfillment of personal, professional, and organizational goals. In helping others to be successful by applying the skills and guidelines presented in *Managing People*, you will not only enhance your effectiveness as a manager, but become a leader that others want to follow.

Chapter 1

Understanding yourself

Knowing yourself will give you valuable insights into your aptitude for managing others. It allows you to understand how you're perceived by others, why they respond to you in the way they do, and how to get the best from them.

Developing self-awareness

Awareness of your emotions, personality, what you enjoy and dislike, what motivates you, and what comes easily or poses challenges is a key precursor to developing effective managerial ability. Quite simply, if you can't manage yourself, you will not be able to manage anyone else.

Keeping moving

The best way to enhance your self-awareness is to learn in a systematic way from your own experiences. Start by reflecting on situations in your working life, your actions in response to them, and the outcomes of these events. Schedule a regular time to do this, either at the beginning or end of a workday, when you are not in the thick of the action. Give yourself space to reflect, and make sure you can be alone and uninterrupted for a significant period of time. Try to gain a better understanding of what happened and think about how you can learn from each situation.

Keeping a journal

Keeping a journal is a good way to help you learn from experience. Journals are similar to diaries, but include entries that address critical aspects of your managerial experiences and reflect on interactions with bosses, employees, and teammates. Such entries can describe a good (or bad) way someone handled a situation; a problem in the making; the different ways people react to situations; or your thoughts on people in the news, or in books or movies. If you want to solicit feedback, post your journal as an online blog.

TIP

MAKE NOTES

Use your journal to "think on paper" about what you have read about management in this or other books, or your experiences in management training programs.

Analyzing your performance

Assessing your progress toward your goals can help you gain a fuller understanding of your strengths and weaknesses. Whenever you make a key decision or take a key action, write down what you expect will happen. Then, every three or four months, compare the actual results with your expectations. If you practice this method consistently, it will help you discover what you are doing, or failing to do, that deprives you of the full benefits of your strengths, and will demonstrate areas in which you are not particularly competent and cannot perform adequately.

 IN FOCUS... FEEDBACK

It is important to have a person in your life who gives you honest, gut-level feedback, to help you gain perspective on your experiences and learn from them. This should be someone you trust enough to go to when you have real problems and ask, "Am I off base here? Am I crazy?"

This person could be a partner, a mentor, a best friend, a co-worker, a therapist, or a personal coach. Today, many organizations are providing their managers with 360-degree feedback, allowing them to receive insights on their strengths and weaknesses from other members of staff.

Using emotional intelligence

Emotional intelligence (EI) is the ability to monitor and work with your and others' emotions. It is measured in EQ, which is the emotional equivalent of IQ. Daniel Goleman—author of the bestselling *Emotional Intelligence*—and other writers suggest that a technically proficient manager with a high EQ will be more successful than a manager who has only a high IQ.

Understanding EQ

Your EQ is the measure of your ability to understand and interact with others and becomes more important the more people you deal with. EQ does not measure personality traits or cognitive capacity. Emotional intelligence can be developed over time and can be improved through training and therapy. Those with a high EQ will be better able to control their own emotions, while at the same time using them as a basis for action. Working with emotions, rather than being at the mercy of them, makes individuals more successful in dealing with the demands of the environment around them. They are better able to control impulses and deal with stress, and better at problem solving. All of these qualities help the individual to perform more competently at work.

CHECKLIST APPLYING EMOTIONAL INTELLIGENCE

	YES	NO
• Am I aware of my feelings and do I act accordingly?	☐	☐
• Can I share my feelings in a straightforward, composed manner?	☐	☐
• Do I treat others with compassion, sensitivity, and kindness?	☐	☐
• Am I open to the opinions and ideas of others?	☐	☐
• Can I decisively confront problem people?	☐	☐
• Do I maintain a balance between my personal life and work?	☐	☐

Managing emotions

Emotional intelligence has two aspects: one inward facing and one outward facing. The first of these is your emotional self-awareness and your ability to manage your own emotions. The second is your degree of empathy, or awareness of others' emotions, and your ability to productively manage relationships with others. Both inward- and outward-facing aspects of emotional intelligence are made up of a number of skills or competencies.

Using EI at work

To be a successful manager in today's business world, a high EQ may be more important than sheer intellectual or technical ability. A manager who leads a project team of diverse people will need to understand and interact successfully with others. Applying emotional intelligence at work means you are open to the ideas of others and can build and mend relationships with others. You are aware of your feelings and act accordingly, articulating ideas so that others can understand them, developing rapport, building trust, and working toward consensus. Managers who are attuned to their own feelings and the feelings of others use this understanding to enhance personal, team, and organizational performance.

The four competencies of emotional intelligence

SELF-AWARENESS
Emotional self-awareness; accurate self-assessment; self-confidence

SELF-MANAGEMENT
Emotional self-control; trustworthiness; conscientiousness; achievement orientation; adaptability; optimism; initiative

SOCIAL AWARENESS
Empathy; organizational awareness; service orientation

RELATIONSHIP MANAGEMENT
Development of others; inspirational leadership; influence; communication; change catalyst; conflict management; bond building; teamwork and collaboration

Applying assertiveness

An effective manager needs to behave in an active and assertive* manner to get things done. Assertive managers are able to express their feelings and act with appropriate degrees of openness and candor, but still have a regard for the feelings or rights of others.

Understanding personality types

*Assertive — being able to make clear statements of what you want from others in a given situation, without being abrasive or demeaning.

Assertiveness and the ability to express your feelings to others are skills that people possess to different extents. Some are aggressive, direct, and blunt, and can appear domineering, pushy, or self-centered. Most people tend to be passive, inhibited, and submissive; they bottle up their feelings and fail even to stand up for their legitimate rights. Passive individuals seek to avoid conflicts and tend to sublimate their own needs and feelings in order to satisfy others.

Most people fall between the extremes of passive and aggressive. At these extremes, passive and aggressive behaviors hinder effective managerial relations because neither encourages openness. Effective managers need to be assertive, express their ideas and feelings openly, and stand up for their rights, and all in a way that makes it easier for those they are managing to do the same. The assertive manager is always sensitive to the needs of others; he or she does not seek to rule less assertive people. Trying to achieve dominance may produce short-term results but will not make the best use of the abilities of members of your team.

ASK YOURSELF... AM I ASSERTIVE ENOUGH?

- Does my response accurately reflect how I feel if I'm given a compliment about my work?
- Am I able to speak up when I'm in a group of strangers?
- If others interrupt me when I am talking, can I hold my ground?
- Do I avoid being taken advantage of by other people?
- Am I able to criticize others' work if I think they might react badly?

Becoming more assertive

STATE YOUR CASE
Try beginning your conversations with "I" phrases, such as "I think," "I believe," or "I need."

BE PREPARED
Prepare for tricky encounters: have all the facts at hand, and try to anticipate the other person's replies.

USE OPEN QUESTIONS
If you are finding it hard to get a person to talk to you, use open questions that cannot be answered with a simple "yes" or "no" answer.

VISUALIZE YOURSELF
Try assertive role play with a trusted colleague, to help you to see yourself as an assertive person.

GET PERSPECTIVE
Try to see a situation from the other person's point of view. Most workplace bullies, for example, are hiding their own insecurities or an inability to do the job. Use this knowledge to give you perspective on any feelings of intimidation or offense you experience, and offer the bully help to overcome their problems.

BE PATIENT
You'll need time and practice to become comfortable with the new behavior. If you are naturally a passive person, recognize that those around you may initially be uncomfortable when you start to become more assertive.

Examining your assumptions

Managers tend to treat their staff according to assumptions they hold about what motivates people. These assumptions create self-fulfilling prophecies in the behavior of the staff. Managers reward what they expect, and consequently only get what they expect. Challenging your own assumptions is one of the first steps in becoming a better manager.

Contrasting X and Y styles

Prominent management theorist Douglas McGregor distinguished two management styles—X and Y—based on the assumptions held by managers about the motives of their staff. X-style managers believe that workers need to be coerced and directed. They tend to be strict and controlling, giving their workers little latitude and punishing poor performance. They use few rewards and typically give only negative feedback. These managers see little point in workers having autonomy, because they think that the workforce neither expects nor desires cooperation.

X AND Y ASSUMPTIONS

X-STYLE MANAGERS	Y-STYLE MANAGERS
Employees inherently dislike work and will attempt to avoid it.	Employees can enjoy work and can view it as being as natural to them as rest or play.
Employees must be coerced, controlled, or threatened with punishment to achieve goals.	People will exercise self-direction and self-control if they are committed to the objectives behind the tasks they are performing.
Employees will shirk responsibility and seek formal direction.	The average person can learn to accept and seek responsibility.
Most workers place security above all other factors associated with work and will display little ambition.	Most workers place job satisfaction and career fulfillment high on their list of priorities.

Y-style assumptions reflect a much more optimistic view of human nature. Y-style management contends that people will gladly direct themselves toward objectives if their efforts are appropriately rewarded. Managers who hold Y assumptions assume a great deal of confidence in their workers. They are less directive and empower workers, giving them more responsibilities and freedom to accomplish tasks as they deem appropriate. They believe that people have hidden potential and the job of the manager is to find and utilize it.

Shaping the environment

Organizations that are designed based on X-style assumptions are very different to those designed by Y-style managers. For example, because they believe that their workers are motivated to help the organization reach its goals, Y-style managers will decentralize authority and give more control to workers than will X-style managers. A Y-style manager realizes that most people are not resistant to organizational needs by nature, but may have become so as a result of negative experiences, and strives to design structures that involve the employees in executing their work roles, such as participative management and joint goal setting. These approaches allow employees to exercise some self-direction and self-control in their work lives.

In Y-style management, although individuals and groups are still accountable for their activities, the role of the manager is not to exert control but to provide support and advice and to make sure that workers have the resources they need to effectively perform their jobs. By contrast, X-style managers consider their role to be to monitor workers to ensure that they contribute to the production process and do not threaten product quality.

TIP

ANALYZE YOURSELF

Honestly review every decision you make and every task you delegate. In each case, ask yourself what you assumed the staff involved would think, and how you expected them to behave. Remember that positive expectations help to produce positive outcomes.

Clarifying your values

Values are stable and enduring beliefs about what is good, right, and worthwhile and about the behavior that is desirable for achieving what is worthwhile. To be an effective manager, it is necessary to have a good understanding of what your values are and to act accordingly.

Defining values

Values are formed early in our lives, from the influence of our parents, teachers, friends, religious leaders, and media role models. Some may change as we go through life and experience different behaviors. Your values manifest themselves in everything you do and the choices that you make. If you are someone who particularly values promptness, for example, you will make sure that you always behave in ways that mean you are on time for appointments. The thought of being late will stimulate feelings of stress in you, and induce a subsequent adrenaline rush as you hurry to be at the appointment on time. As a manager, it is important for you to clarify your values, so that you can determine what your goals are and how you want to manage yourself and others to achieve them.

ASK YOURSELF... ABOUT YOUR INFLUENCES

- Who are the individuals and what are the events that influenced the development of my value system?
- Are these sources of influence still as important to me as recent events and people who influence me now?
- Are my values still appropriate as guides of behavior in the world I live in today?
- Should I consider changing some of my values to make them more relevant?

Clarifying your personal values

It may sound strange, but one of the best ways to clarify your personal values and gain a clear understanding of what is important to you is to think about how you would like to be remembered in your eulogy. Sit quietly and consider how you want your friends and family to remember you, and what you want your work colleagues to say they thought of you. Also think of your broader contributions—how would you like to be remembered in the communities you are a part of? Make notes, and use the information you write down to identify the values that are most important to you.

Dealing with conflicts

It can be challenging when your personal values conflict with those of your organization, or when there are conflicting values between individuals or sub-groups. Value differences can exist, for example, about how to perform jobs, the nature of reward systems, or the degree of intimacy in work relationships. Having a clear understanding of your own personal value set will help you to manage these conflict situations. If you are clear about your own values, you can act with integrity and practice what you preach regardless of emotional or social pressure. To address a conflict situation, first make sure you are aware of, understand, and are tolerant of the value differences held by the other parties. This will help you to determine whether the value conflict is, in fact, irresolvable and will require personnel changes, or whether compromises and adjustments can be made to accommodate the different perspectives.

 IN FOCUS...
TYPES OF VALUE

Values can be classified into two types: terminal and instrumental. Terminal values (your "ends" in life) are desirable ends or goals, such as a comfortable, prosperous life, world peace, great wisdom, or salvation. Instrumental values (the "means" to those ends) are beliefs about what behaviors are appropriate in striving for desired goals and ends. Consider a manager who works extra hours to help deliver a customer's rush order. The attitude displayed is a willingness to help a customer with a problem. The value that serves as the foundation of this attitude might be that of service to others.

Developing your personal mission statement

A personal mission statement provides you with the long-term vision and motivation to manage yourself and others in your team according to your own values. It also allows you to establish your purpose and goals as a manager. Regular evaluation of your performance, based on your mission statement, inspires good self-management.

Defining your future

Your personal mission statement spells out your managerial philosophy. It defines the type of manager you want to be (your character), what you want to accomplish (your contributions), and what principles guide your behavior (your values). It provides you with the vision and values to direct your managerial life—the basis for setting long- and short-term goals, and how best to deploy your time.

LEARN FROM SETBACKS

Things will not always work out as you have planned. When you experience setbacks, be honest with yourself about what happened and why, and think carefully about whether you need to re-evaluate your goals.

Setting out your philosophy

Make sure that your personal mission statement is an accurate reflection of your values, goals, and aspirations for success. A personal statement might read: "My career goals are to effectively manage my team to achieve respect and knowledge, to use my talents as a manager to help others, and to play an active role in this organization." Another individual's statement might have a very different focus: "As a manager in this creative firm, I want to establish a fault-free, self perpetuating learning environment." Re-evaluate your statement on a regular basis— annually, at least—to ensure that it still describes your overall vision for your future as a manager.

BE SMART
Set goals that are Specific, Measurable, Attainable, Realistic, and Time-bound. You are much more likely to achieve goals that are well defined and within your reach.

SET YOUR GOALS
Personalize your goals. You will be far more committed to goals that you have set yourself, rather than those that have been set for you by someone else.

SEE THE FUTURE
Develop a vision of what it will be like when you achieve your goals. Your vision of a desirable future can be a powerful motivating force.

Setting and attaining your personal managerial goals

UP

GET SUPPORT
Develop a support group of people who will help you in achieving your goals. Your support group should include those with the resources you need to be successful.

REWARD YOURSELF
Reward yourself for small wins. When you achieve incremental progress toward your goals, treat yourself to a reward, such as a night out or some recreational activity.

EVALUATE PROGRESS
Continually evaluate your performance against your mission statement. When things do not work out, be honest with yourself about why.

Chapter 2

Interacting with others

Your effectiveness as a manager is defined by your ability to interact with other people. A manager needs to guide others through careful communication, teaching, and assessment to work to their full potential, both individually and as a team.

Communicating effectively

It is easy to see investment in communication as a luxury, especially in times of economic adversity. However, good communication is a proven tool for improving commitment in those you are managing, and so for boosting revenue and product quality.

Getting your message across

Communication is the process of sending a message to another person with the intent of evoking an outcome or a change in behavior. It is more efficient when it uses less time and fewer resources; it is effective when the information is conveyed exactly as you intend. Good communication means balancing the two: for example, explaining a new procedure to each staff member individually may be less efficient than calling a meeting where everyone can hear about it. However, if staff members have very disparate sets of interests, one-to-one coaching may be more effective.

Delivering messages

The components of the communication process are the sender, the receiver, the message, and the channel. First, the message is encoded into a format that will get the idea across. Then it is transmitted through the most appropriate channel. This is chosen on the basis of efficiency and effectiveness, as well as practical factors, such as the need to produce a stable record of the communication; whether the information needs to be kept confidential; speed and cost; and the complexity of the communication.

Channels can be oral (speeches, meetings, phone calls, presentations, or informal discussions); written (letters, memoranda, reports, or manuals); electronic (emails, text messages, podcasts, video conferences, websites, or webcasts); or non-verbal (touch, facial expression, or intonation). Finally, the message must be successfully decoded by the receiver. Many factors may intrude, preventing the receiver from correctly understanding what they are told. These range from semantics or different word interpretations to different frames of reference, cultural attitudes, and mistrust.

Before you send a message, ask yourself how much you understand about it, and what is the level of the recipient's understanding? Will the recipient understand the language and jargon you use, and do they have technology that is compatible with yours?

REDUCE "NOISE"

Noise is anything that interferes, at any stage, with the communication process. The ultimate success of the communication process depends to a large degree on overcoming noise, so make an effort to keep your messages clear, concise, and to the point.

CASE STUDY

Tom's of Maine

Tom Chappell is the founder of Tom's of Maine, a successful natural toothpaste and health company in the US. Chappell is a strong believer in using face-to-face communication to deal with rumors, morale issues, and other communication problems. Every month, he meets informally with his employees and talks about the company's performance and future plans, and solicits feedback from every member of his staff. He says that the best way to deal with employee communication is to be honest and forthright, share information, and "tell it like it is."

Sending messages

Effective communication with those you are managing requires that you send clear and comprehensible messages that will be understood as you intend them to be. You can transmit messages more effectively by making them clearer and developing your credibility.

TIP

BE CONSISTENT
Ensure that your messages are congruent with your actions. Saying one thing and doing another is confusing and creates distrust.

Getting your point across

To be successful, every manager must develop the ability to send clear, unambiguous messages that efficiently convey the information they want to deliver. Effective messages use multiple channels to get the information across; for example, if you match your facial and body gestures to the intended meaning of a message while drawing a diagram to explain it, you are using three channels. Make sure that you take responsibility for the feelings and evaluations in your messages, using personal pronouns such as "I" and "mine." Make the information in your messages specific, and refer to concrete details to avoid the possibility of misinterpretation. Keep your language simple, and avoid technical jargon.

Hitting the right tone

"I need the report delivered by 4.30pm on Friday afternoon."

"I'm not happy when you're late for meetings."

"I need the report delivered as soon as possible."

"Everyone feels you're not pulling your weight."

✔ CHECKLIST **COMMUNICATING**
USING EFFECTIVE MESSAGES

	YES	NO
• Do I use multiple channels when sending messages?	☐	☐
• Do I provide all relevant information?	☐	☐
• Am I complete and specific?	☐	☐
• Do I use "I" statements to claim my messages as my own?	☐	☐
• Am I congruent in my verbal and nonverbal messages?	☐	☐
• Do I use language that the receiver can understand?	☐	☐
• Do I obtain feedback to ensure that my message has been understood and not misinterpreted?	☐	☐

Being credible

Sender credibility is reflected in the recipient's belief that the sender is trustworthy. To increase your sender credibility, ensure that you:

• Know what you are talking about: recipients are more attentive when they perceive that senders have expertise.

• Establish mutual trust: owning up to your motives can eliminate the recipient's anxiety about your intentions.

• Share all relevant information: senders are seen as unethical when they intentionally provoke receivers into doing things they would not have done if they had had all of the information.

• Be honest: one of the key things people want in a leader and co-worker is honesty. As a sender, avoid any form of deception, which is the conscious alteration of information to influence another's perceptions.

• Be reliable: if you are dependable, predictable, and consistent, recipients will perceive you as being trustworthy.

• Be warm, friendly, and supportive: this will give you more personal credibility than a posture of hostility, arrogance, or abruptness.

• Be dynamic: being confident, dynamic, and positive in your delivery of information will make you seem more credible than someone who is passive, withdrawn, and unsure.

• Make appropriate self-disclosures: responsibly revealing your feelings, reactions, needs, and desires to others is essential when establishing supportive relationships. It facilitates congruency, builds trust and credibility, and helps recipients of your messages develop empathy and understanding with you.

Listening actively

Many communication problems develop because listening skills are ignored, forgotten, or taken for granted. Active listening is making sense of what you hear. It requires paying attention and interpreting all verbal, visual, and vocal stimuli presented to you.

Understanding the basics

Active listening has four essential ingredients: concentration, empathy, acceptance, and taking responsibility for completely understanding the message. To listen actively, you must concentrate intensely on what the speaker is saying and tune out competing miscellaneous thoughts that create distractions. Try to understand what the speaker

LISTENING WELL

FAST TRACK	OFF TRACK
Keeping an open mind, free from preconceived ideas	Judging the value of the speaker's ideas by appearance and delivery
Giving the speaker your full attention while they are talking	Thinking about what you are going to say while the speaker is talking
Assessing the full meaning behind the words that are being spoken	Listening for specific facts rather than the overall message
Asking questions when you need more information	Interrupting the speaker when you have a better idea
Withholding judgement until the speaker has finished talking	Always trying to have the last word

wants to communicate rather than what you want to understand. Listen objectively and resist the urge to start evaluating what the person is saying, or you may miss the rest of the message. Finally, do whatever is necessary to get the full, intended meaning from the speaker's message—listen for feelings and content, and ask questions to ensure you have understood.

Employing the techniques

Active listening is hard work and starts with your own personal motivation. If you are unwilling to exert the effort to hear and understand, no amount of additional advice is going to improve your listening effectiveness. If you are motivated to become an effective listener, there are a number of specific techniques you can use to improve your skills:

• Make eye contact: this focuses your attention, reduces the likelihood that you will become distracted, and encourages the speaker.

• Show interest: use nonverbal signals, such as head nods, to convey to the speaker that you're listening.

• Avoid distracting actions: looking at your watch or shuffling papers are signs that you aren't fully attentive and might be missing part of the message.

• Take in the whole picture: interpret feelings and emotions as well as factual content.

• Ask questions: seek clarification if you don't understand something. This also reassures the speaker that you're listening to them.

• Paraphrase: restate what the speaker has said in your own words with phrases such as "What I hear you saying is…" or "Do you mean…?"

• Don't interrupt: let speakers complete their thoughts before you try to respond.

• Confront your biases: use information about speakers to improve your understanding of what they are saying, but don't let your biases distort the message.

SET THE CONTEXT

Mentally summarize and integrate what a speaker says, and put each new bit of information into the context of what has preceded it.

Reading nonverbal cues

Nonverbal communication is made up of visual, vocal, and tactile signals and the use of time, space, and image. As much as 93 percent of the meaning that is transmitted in face-to-face communication can come from nonverbal channels, so you should be aware of these cues.

Decoding the truth

The visual part of nonverbal communication is often called body language. It includes expressions, eye movement, posture, and gestures. The face is the best communicator of nonverbal messages. By "reading" a person's facial expression, we can detect unvocalized feelings. Appearance is important, too—people do judge a book by its cover, and most of us react favorably to an expected image. In terms of dress, color can convey meaning (brown can convey trust; dark colors, power), as does style (pure fibers such as wool or silk suggest higher status). Posture is important—a relaxed posture, such as sitting back with legs stretched out and hands behind the head, signals confidence.

If a person says one thing but communicates something different through intonation and body language, tension and distrust can arise; the receiver will typically choose the nonverbal interpretation because it is more reliable than the verbal. For example, if you ask your boss when you will be eligible for a promotion and she looks out of the window, covers a yawn, and says, "I would say you might have a chance in the not-too-distant future," you should not count on being promoted soon.

NERVOUSNESS
Clearing one's throat, covering the mouth while speaking, fidgeting, shifting weight from one foot to the other, tapping fingers, pacing.

BOREDOM OR IMPATIENCE
Drumming fingers, foot swinging, brushing or picking at lint, doodling, or looking at one's watch.

Feelings that can be read from gestures and body language

OPENNESS
Holding hands in an open position, having an unbuttoned coat or collar, removing one's coat, moving closer, leaning slightly forward, and uncrossing arms and legs.

DEFENSIVENESS
Holding body rigid, with arms or legs tightly crossed, eyes glancing sideways, minimal eye contact, lips pursed, fists clenched, and a downcast head.

CONFIDENCE, SUPERIORITY, AND AUTHORITY
Using relaxed and expansive gestures, such as leaning back with fingers laced behind the head and hands together at the back with chin thrust upward.

Teaching skills

As a manager, an important part of your role is to help those you are managing to develop their skills. If you can encourage the development of skills such as self-awareness, communication, and time management, you will be rewarded with a high-performing team.

HOW TO... TEACH NEW SKILLS

Help the learner to form a conceptual understanding of a new skill.

↓

Plan how they can test their understanding of the skill.

↓

Get the learner to apply the new skill in concrete experience.

↓

Observe what happened and discuss ways in which they can improve.

Learning by experience

People learn faster and retain more information if they have to exert some kind of active effort. The famous quote, attributed to Confucius: "I hear and I forget. I see and I remember. I do and I understand" is frequently used to support the value of learning through experience. A major implication of this notion is that new skills can be learned only through experimenting with new behaviors, observing the results, and learning from the experience. The learning of new skills is maximized when learners get the opportunity to combine watching, thinking, and doing. The experiential learning model encompasses four elements: learning new concepts (conceptualizing), planning how to test the ideas (plan to test), actively applying the skill in a new experience (gaining concrete experience), and examining the consequences of the experience (reflective observation). After reflecting on the experience, the learner uses the lessons they have learned from what happened to create a refined conceptual map of the skill, and the cycle continues.

To use the experiential learning model to teach skills, you need to: ensure that the learner understands the skill both conceptually and behaviorally; give them opportunities to practice it; give feedback on how well they are performing the skill; and encourage them to use the skill often enough so that it becomes integrated into their behavioral repertoire.

EFFECTIVE APPROACHES TO TEACHING SKILLS

APPROACH	WHY IT WORKS
Being prepared Knowing ahead of time what you want the outcome of your skills training to be.	Unless you know where you want things to go, you won't know how to conduct yourself to get there.
Listening Keeping communication lines open and indicating to others that their opinions are important.	The key to effectively teaching a skill is often expressed by the learner, but overlooked by the manager when they fail to hear it.
Using questions Presenting a concept, options for applying it, and the consequences, then asking the learner what they will do.	Asking rather than telling an employee how best to apply a new skill shows respect, and, because it allows them to think it through for themselves, it helps them to learn faster.
Being positive Correcting mistakes in a positive way, not in one that is patronizing or makes others feel worthless and inferior.	Using positive messages, such as "I can see that you want to do well and I think that I can help you learn to do better," will help to motivate the person you are teaching.
Being honest and upfront Making it clear to the learner what is really required of them, and why this is important.	People will be more willing to accept your skill teaching if they trust and respect you because they will believe you are honest and forthright.
Setting performance targets Indicating the acceptable level of performance you expect from those you are teaching, and holding them to it.	In the long run, people will respect you more if you hold them to a standard of performance, as they will know any praise they receive from you is sincere and deserved.

Inspiring others

When you endeavor to teach new skills to others, you are attempting to motivate specific behavior changes in them. This is more effective if you can convince those you are teaching that, by acting as you suggest, they will gain something that they value. Successful teaching requires you to inspire others to want to cooperate with you. However, different people consider different skills to be more or less valuable to them, so you will also discover that the majority of responsibility for the learning of a new skill rests with the person you are teaching. Learners who really want to improve their skills and are willing to put in the effort will be successful.

Giving feedback

Most managers will enthusiastically give their employees positive feedback but often avoid or delay giving negative feedback, or substantially distort it, for fear of provoking a defensive reaction. However, improving employees' performance depends on balanced and considered feedback.

Valuing feedback

Providing regular feedback to your employees will improve their performance. This is because:
• Feedback can induce a person to set goals, which act as motivators of their performance.
• Feedback tells the person how well they are progressing toward those goals. Positive feedback gives reinforcement, while constructive negative feedback can result in increased effort.
• The content of the feedback will suggest ways that the person can improve their performance.
• Providing feedback demonstrates to a person that you care about how they are doing.

As a rule, positive feedback is usually accepted readily, while negative feedback often meets resistance. When preparing to deliver negative feedback, first make sure you are aware of any conflict that could arise and think about how to deal with it. Ensure that negative feedback comes from a credible source, that it is objective, and that it is supported by hard data such as quantitative performance indicators and specific examples.

TALK ABOUT THE JOB
Keep feedback job-related. Never make personal judgements, such as "You are stupid and incompetent."

GIVE DETAIL
Avoid vague statements such as "You have a bad attitude" or "I'm impressed with the job you did." The recipient needs to understand exactly what they have or haven't done well.

How to provide feedback

USE GOALS
Keep feedback goal-oriented. It's purpose is not to unload your feelings on someone.

BE NON-JUDGMENTAL
Keep feedback descriptive and fair rather than judgmental.

MAKE IT ATTAINABLE
When delivering negative feedback, make sure you only criticize shortcomings over which the person has some control.

EXPLAIN YOUR REASONS
Explain to the recipient why you are being critical or complimentary about specific aspects of their performance.

ENSURE A GOOD FIT
Tailor the feedback to fit the person. Consider past performance and future potential in designing the frequency, amount, and content of performance feedback.

CHECK UNDERSTANDING
Once you have given your feedback, have the recipient rephrase the content to check that they have fully understood what you have said and are taking away the right message from your feedback session.

Negotiating

Negotiation is a process by which two or more parties exchange goods or services and attempt to agree upon the exchange rate for them. Managers spend a lot of time negotiating, and need to be able to do it well. They have to negotiate salaries for incoming employees, cut deals with superiors, bargain over budgets, work out differences with associates, and resolve conflicts between members of their team.

Understanding approaches

There are two general approaches to negotiation: distributive and integrative bargaining. Distributive bargaining assumes zero-sum conditions, that is: "Any gain I make is at your expense," and vice versa. Integrative bargaining assumes a win–win solution is possible. Each is appropriate in different situations.

Distributive bargaining tactics focus on getting an opponent to agree to a deal that meets your specific goals. Such tactics include persuading opponents of the impossibility of getting their needs met in other ways or the advisability of accepting your offer; arguing that your position is fair, while theirs is not; and trying to get the other party to feel emotionally generous toward you and accept an outcome that meets your goals.

CASE STUDY

A win–win solution
After closing a $15,000 order from a small clothing retailer, sales rep Deb Hansen called in the order to her firm's credit department, and was told that the firm could not approve credit for this customer because of a past slow-pay record. The next day, Deb and the firm's credit supervisor met to discuss the problem. Deb did not want to lose the business; neither did the credit supervisor, but he also didn't want to get stuck with a bad debt. The two openly reviewed their options. After considerable discussion, they agreed on a solution: the credit supervisor would approve the sale, but the clothing store's owner would provide a bank guarantee that would assure payment if the bill was not paid within 60 days.

Finding solutions

Integrative, or win–win, bargaining is generally preferable to distributive bargaining. Distributive bargaining leaves one party a loser, and so it tends to build animosities and deepen divisions between people. On the other hand, integrative bargaining builds long-term relationships and facilitates working together in the future. It bonds negotiators and allows each to leave the bargaining table feeling that he or she has achieved a victory. For integrative bargaining to work, however, both parties must openly share all information, be sensitive to each other's needs, trust each other, and remain flexible.

Negotiating well

Careful attention to a few key guidelines can increase a manager's odds of successful negotiation outcomes. Always start by considering the other party's point of view. Acquire as much information as you can about their interests and goals. Always go into a negotiation with a concrete strategy. Treat negotiations the way expert players treat the game of chess, always knowing ahead of time how they will respond to any given situation.

HOW TO... NEGOTIATE

Begin with a positive overture, and establish rapport and mutual interests.

⬇

Make a small concession early on if you can. Concessions tend to be reciprocated and can lead to a quick agreement.

⬇

Concentrate on the issues, not on the personal characteristics or personality of your opponent.

⬇

If your opponent attacks you or gets emotional, let them blow off steam without taking it personally.

⬇

Pay little attention to initial offers, treating them as merely starting points.

⬇

Focus on the other person's interests and your own goals and principles while you generate other possibilities.

⬇

Emphasize win–win solutions to the negotiation.

⬇

Make your decisions based on principles and results, not emotions or pressure.

Managing conflict

Conflict is natural to organizations and can never be completely eliminated. If not managed properly, conflict can be dysfunctional and lead to undesirable consequences, such as hostility, lack of cooperation, and even violence. When managed effectively, conflict can stimulate creativity, innovation, and change.

Understanding the causes

PUT YOURSELF IN THEIR SHOES
Empathize with the other parties in the conflict, and try to understand their values, personality, feelings, and resources. Make sure you know what is at stake for them.

Conflicts exist whenever an action by one party is perceived as preventing or interfering with the goals, needs, or actions of another party. Conflicts have varying causes but are generally rooted in one of three areas: problems in communication; disagreements over work design, policies, and practices; and personal differences.

Disagreements frequently arise from semantic difficulties, misunderstandings, poor listening, and noise in the communication channels. Communication breakdowns are inevitable in work settings, often causing workers to focus on placing blame on others instead of trying to solve problems.

Conflicts can also result when people or groups disagree over goal priorities, decision alternatives, performance criteria, and resource allocations. The things that people want, such as promotions, pay increases, and office space, are scarce resources that must be divided up. Ambiguous rules, regulations, and performance standards can also create conflicts.

Individual idiosyncrasies and differences in personal value systems originating from different cultural backgrounds, education, experience, and training often lead to conflicts. Stereotyping, prejudice, ignorance, and misunderstanding may cause people who are different to be perceived by some to be untrustworthy adversaries.

Handling conflict

There are five basic approaches managers can use to try to resolve conflicts. Each has strengths and weaknesses, so choose the one most appropriate to your situation:

• Avoidance: not every conflict requires an assertive action. Avoidance works well for trivial conflicts or if emotions are running high and opposing parties need time to cool down.

• Accommodation: if you need to maintain a harmonious relationship, you may choose to concede your position on an issue that is much more important to the other party.

• Competition: satisfying your own needs at the expense of other parties is appropriate when you need a quick resolution on important issues, or where an unpopular action must be taken.

• Compromise: this works well when the parties are equal in power, or when you need a quick solution or a temporary solution to a complex issue.

• Collaboration: use this when the interests of all parties are too important to be ignored. Discuss the issues openly and honestly with all parties, listen actively, and make a careful deliberation over a full range of alternatives.

Approaches to conflict-handling

	UNCOOPERATIVE	COOPERATIVE
ASSERTIVE	**COMPETITION** Using your formal authority to resolve issues the way you want.	**COLLABORATION** Finding a solution that is advantageous to all parties.
	COMPROMISE Each party gives up something to reach a solution that is satisfactory to all.	
UNASSERTIVE	**AVOIDANCE** Withdrawing or postponing the conflict.	**ACCOMMODATION** Yielding to another party's position.

Valuing diversity

Understanding and managing people who are similar to us can be challenging, but understanding and managing those who are dissimilar from us and from each other is tougher. As the workplace becomes more diverse and as business becomes more global, managers must understand how cultural diversity affects the expectations and behavior of everyone in the organization.

TIP

LET EVERYONE KNOW

Make a public commitment to valuing diversity—this will ensure that you are accountable for your actions, and may attract potential employees who prefer to work for someone who values equal opportunities for all.

Understanding the changes

The labor market is dramatically changing. Most countries are experiencing an increase in the age of their workforce, increased immigration, and, in many, a rapid increase in the number of working women. The globalization of business also brings with it a cross-cultural mandate. With more businesses selling and manufacturing products and services abroad, managers increasingly see the need to ensure that their employees can relate to customers from many different cultures. Rich McGinn, of US telecommunications giant Lucent Technologies, said: "We are in a war for talent. And the only way you can meet your business imperatives is to have all people as part of your talent pool." Workers who believe that their differences are not merely tolerated but valued by their employer are more likely to be loyal, productive, and committed.

Capitalizing on diversity

Managers face many challenges capitalizing on diversity, such as: coping with employees' unfamiliarity with native languages, learning which rewards are valued by different ethnic groups, and providing career development programs that fit the values of different ethnic groups. There are several ways for you to try to capitalize on diversity:

• Communicate your objectives and expectations about diversity to employees through a range of channels, such as vision and mission statements, value statements, slogans, creeds, newsletters, speeches, emails, and everyday conversations.

• Recruit through non-traditional sources. Relying on current employee referrals usually produces a limited range of candidates. Try instead to identify novel sources for recruitment, such as women's job networks, ethnic newspapers, training centers for the disabled, urban job banks, and over-50s clubs.

• Use diverse incentives for motivation. Most studies on motivation are by North American researchers on North American workers. Consequently, these studies are based on beliefs that most people work to promote their own well-being and get ahead. This may be at odds with people from more collectivist countries, such as Venezuela, Singapore, Japan, and Mexico, where individuals are driven by their loyalty to the organization or society, not their own self-interest.

TIP

PRACTICE WHAT YOU PREACH

First look into your heart and mind and root out any prejudice. Then, demonstrate your acceptance in everything that you say and do.

Chapter 3
Managing a team

Teams are the cornerstones of most public and nonprofit organizations. Successful team leaders understand what makes a team effective and what can lead to failure. To be a successful manager, you need to be able to plan and design the work of your team, delegate tasks effectively, monitor progress, and motivate your team to excel.

Setting goals and planning

Planning is a key skill for any manager and starts with having a good understanding of the organization's objectives. It involves establishing a strategy for achieving those goals using the personnel available, and developing the means to integrate and coordinate necessary activities.

Knowing your goals

Planning is concerned with ends (what needs to be done) and means (how those ends are to be achieved). In order to create a plan, managers must first identify the organization's goals—what it is trying to achieve. Goals are the foundation of all other planning activities. They refer to the desired outcomes for the entire organization, for groups and teams within the organization, and for individuals. Goals provide the direction for all management decisions and form the criteria against which actual accomplishments can be measured.

Setting your goals

There are five basic rules that can help you set effective goals. Always make your goals SMART: Specific, Measurable, Aligned, Reachable, and Time-bound.

• **Specific** Goals are meaningful only when they are specific enough to be measured and verified.

• **Measurable** Goals need to have a clear outcome that can be objectively assessed. They also need to have clear benchmarks that can be checked along the way.

• **Aligned** Goals should contribute to the mission, vision, and strategic plan of the organization and be congruent with the values and objectives of the employee implementing them.

• **Reachable** Goals should require you to stretch to reach them, but not be set unrealistically high.

• **Time-bound** Open-ended goals can be neglected because there is no sense of urgency to complete them. Whenever possible, goals should include a specific time limit for accomplishment.

HOW TO... DEVELOP AND IMPLEMENT A PLAN

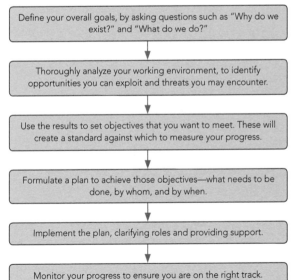

Define your overall goals, by asking questions such as "Why do we exist?" and "What do we do?"

↓

Thoroughly analyze your working environment, to identify opportunities you can exploit and threats you may encounter.

↓

Use the results to set objectives that you want to meet. These will create a standard against which to measure your progress.

↓

Formulate a plan to achieve those objectives—what needs to be done, by whom, and by when.

↓

Implement the plan, clarifying roles and providing support.

↓

Monitor your progress to ensure you are on the right track.

TIP

LOOK TO THE FUTURE

Write down three SMART goals that you want your team to achieve in the next five years, and then plan how you will reach them.

Designing work

Job design refers to the way tasks are combined to form complete jobs. It involves trying to shape the right jobs to conform to the right people, taking into account both the organization's goals and the employees' satisfaction. Well-designed jobs lead to high motivation, high-quality performance, high satisfaction, and low absenteeism and turnover.

TIP

GET THE RIGHT PERSON FOR THE JOB

It is very difficult to completely change how a person performs, so try to match people to jobs that they are good at. This will make them most likely to achieve good results.

Defining jobs

Jobs vary considerably: a lifeguard, for example, will have very different day-to-day responsibilities than an accountant or a builder. However, any job can be described in terms of five core job dimensions:

• Skill variety: the degree to which a job requires a variety of different activities so that the worker can employ a number of different skills and talents.

• Task identity: the degree to which a job requires completion of a whole and identifiable piece of work.

• Task significance: the degree to which a job has an impact on the lives of other people.

• Autonomy: the degree to which a job provides freedom and discretion to the worker in scheduling their tasks and in determining how the work will be carried out.

• Feedback: the degree to which the worker gets direct and clear information about the effectiveness of his or her performance.

As a manager, you can maximize your team's performance by enhancing these five dimensions. Skill variety, task identity, and task significance combine to create meaningful work. Jobs with these characteristics will be perceived as important, valuable, and worthwhile. Jobs that possess autonomy give workers a sense of responsibility for their results. Jobs that provide feedback indicate to the employee how effectively he or she is performing.

Ways to design work by enhancing the five dimensions

1 COMBINE TASKS
Put existing fragmented tasks together to form larger modules of work. This can help to increase skill variety and task identity.

2 CREATE NATURAL WORK UNITS
Design tasks to form an identifiable whole to increase employee "ownership" and to encourage workers to view their jobs as important.

3 ESTABLISH CLIENT RELATIONSHIPS
Building direct relationships between the worker and the client—the user of the product or the service that the employee works on—increases skill variety

4 EXPAND JOBS VERTICALLY
Giving employees responsibilities formerly reserved for managers closes the gap between the "doing" and "controlling" aspects of the job, and increases autonomy.

5 IMPROVE FEEDBACK CHANNELS
Feedback tells employees how well they are performing, and whether their performance is improving, deteriorating, or remaining constant. Employees should receive feedback directly as they do their jobs.

High-performing teams

As Lee Iacocca, former CEO of Chrysler Corporation, said: "All business operations can be reduced to three words: people, product, and profit. People come first. Unless you've got a good team, you can't do much with the other two." Successful managers are those who create, work with, and manage successful teams.

Defining high-performing teams

A team is two or more people who meet regularly, perceive themselves as a distinct entity distinguishable from others, have complementary skills, and are committed to a common purpose, a set of performance goals, and an approach for which they hold themselves mutually accountable. High-performing teams engage in collective work produced by coordinated joint efforts that result in more than the sum of the individual efforts. Teams of 10 or fewer members find it easiest to interact constructively and reach agreement.

Understanding team performance

WHO ARE WE?
Sharing strengths, weaknesses, work preferences, and values allows the establishment of a set of common beliefs for the team, creating a group identity and a feeling of "what we stand for."

WHERE ARE WE NOW?
Understanding the current position means that a team can reinforce its strengths, improve on its weaknesses, and identify opportunities to capitalize on and threats to be aware of.

WHERE ARE WE GOING?
Teams need to have a vision of the pot of gold at the end of the rainbow. They also need a mission, a purpose, and a set of specific team goals that they are all excited about.

HOW WILL WE GET THERE?
Team members must understand who will do what and when to accomplish team goals, and must be clear about their job description, roles on the team, responsibilities, and areas of authority and accountability.

WHAT SUPPORT DO WE GET/NEED?
Reviewing each member's training and development needs can set the stage for individual training, counselling, and mentoring that will strengthen both the individual and the team.

HOW EFFECTIVE ARE WE?
Regular performance reviews of quantity and quality outputs and the team process—with recognition and reward for success—ensure achievement of team goals and provide members with standards.

IN FOCUS... MUTUAL TRUST

A climate of mutual trust is essential in a high-performing team—each member of the team needs to know they can depend on the others. Successful managers build mutual trust by creating a climate of openness in which employees are free to discuss problems without fear of retaliation. They are approachable and respectful and listen to team members' ideas, and develop a reputation for being fair, objective, and impartial in their treatment of others. Consistency and honesty are key, so they avoid erratic and unpredictable behavior and always follow through on any explicit and implied promises they make. Communication is at the heart of building and maintaining mutual interdependence between members of a team. Managers of high-performing teams keep team members informed about upper-management decisions and policies and give accurate feedback on their performance. They are also open and candid about their own problems and limitations.

TIP

CHANGE PERSONNEL

If your teams get bogged down in their own inertia or internal fighting, rotate the members. Consider how certain personalities will mesh and re-form your teams in ways that will better complement skills.

Achieving good teamwork

To help your teams perform to the best of their ability, create clear goals. All team members need to have a thorough understanding of the goals of the team and a belief that these goals embody a worthwhile result. This encourages team members to sublimate personal concerns to those of the team. Members need to be committed to the team's goals, know what they are expected to accomplish, and understand how they will work together to achieve these goals.

However, these goals must be attainable; team members can lose morale if it seems that they are not. To avoid this, set smaller interim milestones in the path to your overall goal. As these smaller goals are attained, your team's success is reinforced. Cohesiveness is increased, morale improves, and confidence builds.

As the manager of a team, it is your job to provide the resources and support that the members need to achieve success. Offer skills training where needed, either personally or by calling in specialists within your organization or outside training services.

Steering your team

Team members should all share in the glory when their team succeeds, and they should share in the blame when it fails. However, members need to know that they cannot ride on the backs of others. Identify what each member's individual contribution to the team's work should be and make it a part of his or her overall performance appraisal.

To help monitor performance, select members of the team to act as participant–observers. While a team is working, the role of the participant–observer is to focus on the processes being used: the sequence of actions that takes place between team members to achieve the team's goal. Periodically, the participant–observer should stop the team from working on its task and discuss the process members are engaged in. The objectives of the participant–observer are to continuously improve the team's functioning by discussing the processes being used and creating strategies for improving them.

Setting standards

Create a performance agreement to record the details of what the team is aiming to achieve, what is required and expected of every team member, and what support will be available to them. Setting out the framework for team success clearly helps to ensure that there is a mutual understanding and common vision of the desired results and emphasizes the standards that you expect from every team member.

✔ **CHECKLIST CREATING A TEAM PERFORMANCE AGREEMENT**

	YES	NO
• Have I identified what is to be done and when?	☐	☐
• Have I specified the boundaries (guiding rules of behavior) or the means for accomplishing results?	☐	☐
• Have I identified the human, financial, technical, or organizational support available to help achieve the results?	☐	☐
• Have I established the standards of performance and the time intervals for evaluation?	☐	☐
• Have I specified what will happen in performance evaluations and the consequences of not meeting the standards?	☐	☐

Delegating effectively

Managers are responsible for getting things done through other people. You need to accomplish assigned goals by delegating responsibility and authority to others. Empowering others through delegation is one of the most powerful managerial tools for increasing productivity.

Empowering others

Managers delegate by transferring authority and responsibility for work to employees. Delegation empowers employees to achieve goals by allowing them to make their own decisions about how to do a job. Delegation also helps develop employees for promotion opportunities by expanding their knowledge, job capabilities, and decision-making skills. Delegation frequently is depicted as having four key components:

- **Allocation of duties** Before a manager can delegate authority, the tasks and activities that need to be accomplished must be explained.
- **Delegation of authority** Delegation is the process of transferring authority to empower a subordinate to act for you as a manager.
- **Assignment of responsibility** Managers should assign responsibility to the empowered employee for performing the job adequately.
- **Creation of accountability** Managers should hold empowered employees responsible for properly carrying out their duties. This includes taking responsibility for the completion of tasks assigned to them and also being accountable to the manager for the satisfactory performance of that work.

Feeling the benefits

Effective delegation is key for any manager. It will free up your time, allowing you to focus on big-picture strategic activities. It can also lead to better decision-making, because it pushes decisions down the organization, meaning that decision-makers are often closer to the problems. It also helps those you are managing develop their own decision-making skills and prepares them for future promotion opportunities.

Letting go

Managers often have trouble delegating. Some are afraid to give up control, explaining, "I like to do things myself, because then I know it's done and it's done right." Others lack confidence in their employees or fear that they may be criticized for others' mistakes. While you may be capable of doing the tasks you delegate better, faster, or with fewer mistakes, it is not possible to do everything yourself. However, you should expect, and accept, some mistakes by those you delegate to. Mistakes are often good learning experiences. You also should put adequate controls and mechanisms for feedback in place so you will know what is happening.

HOW TO...
DELEGATE

CLARIFY THE ASSIGNMENT
Explain what is being delegated, the results you expect, and the timeframe.

↓

SET BOUNDARIES
Ensure that the delegatees understand precisely what the parameters are of the authority you are bestowing on them.

↓

ENCOURAGE PARTICIPATION
Involve delegatees in decisions about what is delegated, how much authority is needed, and standards to be attained.

↓

INFORM OTHERS
Let everyone who may be affected know what has been delegated to whom and how much authority has been granted.

↓

ESTABLISH CONTROLS
Agree on a specific time for completion of the task, and set dates when progress will be checked and problems discussed.

↓

ENCOURAGE DEVELOPMENT
Insist from the beginning that when delegatees come to you with a problem, they also bring a possible solution.

Motivating others

Every day, people make decisions about how much effort to put into their work. Managers have many opportunities to influence these decisions and motivate their team by providing challenging work, recognizing outstanding performance, allowing participation in decisions that affect employees, and showing concern for personal issues.

Understanding needs

As a manager, you need to understand what drives your team to do the best that they can. American psychologist Abraham Maslow proposed that every individual has a five-level hierarchy of needs that they are driven to attempt to satisfy. Once a lower-level need has been largely satisfied, its impact on a person's behavior diminishes, and they begin to be motivated to gain the next highest level need.

There are two aspects to what makes a person perform well: ability and motivation. Ability is the product of aptitude, training, and resources, while motivation is the product of desire and commitment. All of these elements are required for high performance levels. If someone is not performing

CASE STUDY

Prioritizing needs
Theresa, a successful technical writer and a single parent, had been earning a good salary and benefits that enabled her to provide for her family's physical well-being: ample food, comfortable housing and clothing, and good medical care. Her company then announced that it was downsizing, and she feared being laid off. This triggered concerns about her safety needs and meant that she became much less concerned about the higher order needs of belonging to a group or her own self-esteem to perform creative and technically accurate work. Rather, she was motivated to do whatever was necessary to ensure that she kept her job or could find a new one. Once Theresa knew that her job was safe, she changed back to having a higher-order need, energizing her behavior.

well, the first question you should ask yourself is: "Is their poor performance the result of a lack of ability or a lack of motivation?" Motivational methods can often be very effective for improving performance, but if the problem is lack of ability, no amount of pressure or encouragement will help. What the person needs is training, additional resources, or a different job.

Maslow's hierarchy of needs

SELF-ACTUALIZATION NEEDS
The highest level is to feel that we are achieving life goals. At work, this means being able to exercise creativity and to develop and fully utilize our skills.

ESTEEM NEEDS
Next, we are motivated by the need for self-esteem and esteem from others, such as recognition for accomplishments and promotion.

SOCIAL NEEDS
Once you feel reasonably secure, social needs begin to take over. At work, this means having good relationships with co-workers and participating in company social functions.

SAFETY NEEDS
Once physiological needs are satisfied, safety needs are aroused. These can be satisfied at work by having job security and safe working conditions, and receiving medical benefits.

PHYSIOLOGICAL NEEDS
Our most basic needs are for physical survival, such as to satisfy hunger or thirst. At work, this is receiving enough pay to buy food and clothing and pay the rent.

Using positive reinforcement

Rewarding progress and success and recognizing achievements are powerful ways to motivate your team. By rewarding someone for doing something right, you positively reinforce that behavior, giving them an incentive for doing it again. There are two basic types of reward: extrinsic and intrinsic. Many people depend on and highly value extrinsic rewards that are externally bestowed, such as praise, a promotion, or a pay raise. Others place a high value on intrinsic rewards, which originate from their own personal feelings about how they performed or the satisfaction that they derive from a job well done.

Rewarding success

Try to understand whether each individual you are managing values intrinsic or extrinsic rewards more highly. If you always praise achievements, for example, a motivated person who excels largely for the feelings of intrinsic satisfaction will probably begin to view you as superficial. The professional may think, "I know I did a superb job on this project. Why is my manager being so condescending?"

People also desire different types of extrinsic rewards. Praise may be perfectly acceptable to the person motivated by affiliation and relationship needs, but may do nothing for the person expecting a more tangible reward, like money. Typical extrinsic rewards are favorable assignments, trips to desirable destinations, tuition reimbursement, pay raises, bonuses, promotions, and office placements.

> **ASK YOURSELF...**
> ## CAN I DRAW ON MY EXPERIENCE?
>
> • Can you think of a coach, teacher, or manager who motivated you to enhance your performance in a particular task?
> • What did they do to motivate you?
> • How did you feel as a result of their actions?
> • Can you recreate their actions or use their approach when trying to motivate your team?

Motivating your team

There are other methods of motivating employees in addition to direct positive reinforcement. These include:

• **Strengthening effort–performance–reward expectancies** To get the best from your team, emphasize the anticipated reward value, whether extrinsic or intrinsic. Make sure that every individual realizes the link between their performance and the rewards. Even if your organization does not provide performance-based pay, you can bestow other extrinsic rewards, such as allocating more favorable job assignments.

• **Giving performance feedback** Provide feedback to demonstrate that you know what the members of your team are doing and to acknowledge improved performance or a job well done. Especially when individuals are unsure of themselves, you should point out ways in which the person is improving. Praising specific accomplishments will help to bolster that person's self-esteem.

• **Providing salient rewards** Employees don't all value the same rewards equally, so try to tailor your rewards to get the most out of each individual.

• **Reinforcing the right behavior** Quite often what managers say they want, what they reward, and what they get from their team are quite different. If you verbally espouse innovation but reward doing things by the book, you are sending mixed signals and reinforcing the wrong behavior. Think carefully about your rewards and what they mean, and make sure that you reinforce behavior that you want to see repeated.

• **Empowering employees to achieve** Empowering the people you are managing, by giving them the authority, information, and tools they need to do their jobs with greater autonomy, can greatly improve their motivation levels.

✅ ## CHECKLIST **MOTIVATING MY TEAM**

	YES	NO
• Do I set clear goals and reward success?	☐	☐
• Am I positively reinforcing successful behavior?	☐	☐
• Are the rewards I give salient to each individual I am managing?	☐	☐
• Have I considered linking pay to performance?	☐	☐
• Have I redesigned jobs to help motivate the people doing them?	☐	☐
• Do I make opportunities to learn available to my team?	☐	☐

Appraising performance

As a manager, you must ensure that objectives are met and also that employees learn how to enhance their performance. Providing structured feedback through the formal performance appraisal process can increase productivity and morale and decrease absenteeism and staff turnover.

TIP

KEEP YOUR OPTIONS OPEN
When giving your appraisal, avoid absolutes such as "always" and "never"—if the person you are appraising can introduce one exception to your statement, it can destroy the entire statement's validity and damage your credibility.

Assessing progress

Giving feedback in a formal way in performance appraisal interviews conveys to those you are managing that you care about how they are doing. Appraisals allow you to set goals and monitor achievement, helping to motivate your team to perform to a higher level. They allow you to tell each individual how well they're progressing, which can reinforce good behavior and extinguish dysfunctional behavior. However, the interview itself should be the final step in the performance appraisal process. Appraisal should be a continuous process, starting with the establishment and communication of performance standards. Continually assess how each individual is performing relative to these standards, and use this information to discuss a person's performance with them in the appraisal interview.

❓ ASK YOURSELF... AM I PREPARED FOR THE APPRAISAL?

- Have I carefully considered the employee's strengths as well as their weaknesses?
- Can I substantiate, with specific examples, all points of praise and criticism?
- Have I thought about any problems that may occur in the appraisal interview?
- Have I considered how I will react to these problems?

Conducting the appraisal interview

Start with the aim of putting the person at ease. Most people don't like to hear their work criticized, so be supportive and understanding and create a helpful and constructive climate. Begin the interview by explaining what will transpire during the appraisal and why. Keep your appraisal goal-oriented, and make sure that your feedback is specific. Vague statements provide little useful information. Where you can, get the person's own perceptions of the problems being addressed—there may be contributing factors that

you are unaware of. Encourage the person to evaluate themselves as much as possible. In a supportive climate, they may acknowledge performance problems independently, thus eliminating your need to raise them. They may also offer viable solutions.

At the end of the interview, ask the recipient to rephrase the content of your appraisal. This will indicate whether or not you have succeeded in communicating your evaluation clearly. Finish by drawing up a future plan of action. Draft a detailed, step-by-step plan for improvement. Include in the plan what needs to be done, by when, and how you will monitor the person's activities.

CONDUCTING APPRAISAL INTERVIEWS

FAST TRACK	**OFF TRACK**
Focusing only on feedback that relates to the person's job	Sharing your feelings about a person's personality
Providing both positive and negative feedback	Focusing your comments only on bad performance
Sharing first-hand observations as evidence	Including rumors and allegations in your appraisal
Being unafraid to criticize the person constructively	Avoiding offending the other person by sugarcoating your criticism

Chapter 4

Leading others

Leadership is the process of providing direction, influencing and energizing others, and obtaining follower commitment to shared organizational goals. Managers need to lead their team, setting ethical boundaries for them to follow, developing a power base for influencing them to change in positive ways, and helping them improve through coaching and mentoring.

Setting ethical boundaries

Few of us would be likely to steal or cheat, but how principled would you be, or should you be, when faced with routine business situations involving ethical choices? As a leader, you need to have a clear understanding of your ethical principles and set a consistent example for your team.

Understanding ethics

Ethics refer to the rules or principles that define right or wrong conduct. In the workplace, acting ethically is not just an abstraction, it is an everyday occurrence. Consider this dilemma: an employee, after some pressure from you, has found another job. You are relieved because you will not have to fire him; his work has been substandard for some time. But your relief turns to dismay when he asks you for a letter of recommendation. Do you say no and run the risk that he will not leave? Or do you write the letter, knowing that you're influencing someone else to take him on?

Being responsible

Ethics is important for everyone in an organization, particularly as some unethical acts are also illegal. Many organizations want employees to behave ethically because such a reputation is good for business, which in turn can mean larger profits. However, acting ethically is especially crucial for managers. The decisions a manager makes set the standard for those they are managing and help create a tone for the organization. If employees believe all are held to high standards, they are likely to feel better about themselves, their colleagues, and their organization.

Developing ethics

The behavior of managers is under more scrutiny than that of other members of staff, and misdeeds can become quickly and widely known, destroying the reputation of the organization. It is important for managers to develop their own ethical boundaries—lines that they and their employees should not cross. To do this, you need to:

• Know and understand your organization's policy on ethics.

• Anticipate unethical conduct. Be alert to situations that may promote unethical behavior. (Under unusual circumstances, even a normally ethical person may be tempted to act out of character.)

• Consider all consequences. Ask yourself questions such as: "What if my actions were described in detail on a local TV news show, or in the newspaper? What if I get caught doing something unethical? Am I prepared to deal with the consequences?"

• Seek opinions from others. They may have been in a similar situation, or at least can listen and be a sounding board for you.

• Do what you truly believe is right. You have a conscience and are responsible for your behavior. You need to be true to your own internal ethical standards. Ask yourself the simple question: "Can I live with what I have decided to do?"

ASK YOURSELF... IS WHAT I'M ABOUT TO DO ETHICAL?

• Why am I doing what I'm about to do?

• What are my true intentions in taking this action?

• Are there any ulterior motives behind my action, such as proving myself to my peers or superiors?

• Will my actions injure someone, physically or emotionally?

• Would I disclose to my boss or my family what I'm about to do?

Ensuring cultural fit

An organization's culture, or personality, refers to the key characteristics that the organization values and that distinguish it from other organizations. Managers need to be aware of organizational culture because they are expected to respond to the dictates of the culture themselves and also to develop an understanding of the culture in those they are managing.

Analyzing organizational culture

The cultural imperatives of an organization are often not written down or even discussed, but all successful managers must learn what to do and what not to do in their organizations. In fact, the better the match between the manager's personal style and the organization's culture, the more successful the manager is likely to be. Founders create culture in three ways. First, they hire and keep employees who think and feel the way they do. Second, founders indoctrinate and socialize these employees to their way of thinking. Third, founders act as role models, and their personality becomes central to the culture of the organization.

Being able to discern an organization's culture is not always a simple task. Many organizations have given little thought to their culture and do not readily display it. To try to find out more about your organization's culture, you might:

• Observe the physical surroundings. Look at signs, pictures, styles of dress, length of hair, the degree of openness among offices, and how those offices are furnished and arranged.

• Listen to the language. For example, do managers use military terms, such as "take no prisoners," and "divide and conquer"? Or do they speak about "intuition," "care," and "our family of customers"?

• Ask different people the same questions and compare their answers. You might ask: how does this company define success? For what are employees most rewarded? Who is on the fast track and what did they do to get there?

Sustaining culture

Managers are responsible for sustaining organizational culture, by helping new employees learn and adapt to it. A new worker, for example, must be taught what behaviors are valued and rewarded by the organization, so that he or she can learn the "system" and gradually assume those behaviors that are appropriate to their role.

CASE STUDY

Keeping culture consistent

At coffee retailer Starbucks, every employee goes through a set of formal classes during their first few weeks on the job. They are taught the history of the firm, coffee-making techniques, and how to explain Starbucks's Italian drink names to baffled customers, and given coffee-tasting classes. The firm's socialization program turns out employees who are well versed in the company's culture and can represent Starbucks's obsession with "elevating the coffee experience" for its customers.

Solving problems

Managerial success depends on making the right decisions at the right times. However, unless you define a problem and identify its root causes, it is impossible to make appropriate decisions about how to solve it. Effective managers know how to gather and evaluate information that clarifies a problem, develop alternatives, and weigh up the implications of a plan before implementing it.

Spotting problems

A problem exists when a situation is not what is needed or desired. A major responsibility for all managers is to maintain a constant lookout for existing or potential problems, and to spot them early before they escalate into serious situations. Managers fulfil this responsibility by keeping channels of communication open, monitoring employees' current performance, and examining deviations from present plans as well as from past experience. Four situations can alert managers to possible problems:
• A deviation from past experience
• A deviation from a set plan
• When other people communicate problems to you
• When competitors start to outperform your team or organization.

The problem-solving process

1 IDENTIFYING
Being conscious of what is going on around you, so you can spot problems early.

2 DEFINING
Making a careful analysis of the problem to be solved, in order to define it as clearly as possible.

Finding solutions

Problem solving involves closing the gap between what is actually taking place and a desired outcome. Once you have identified a problem that needs to be addressed, start by analyzing the problem and defining it as clearly as you can. This is a key step: the definition you generate will have a major impact on all remaining steps in the process. If you get the definition wrong, all remaining steps will be distorted, because you will base them on insufficient or erroneous information. Definition is important even if the solution appears to be obvious—without a full assessment you may miss an alternative resolution that is more advantageous.

Gather as much information about the situation as you can. Try to understand the goals of all of the parties involved, and clarify any aspects of the problem you are unclear about.

Once you are satisfied that you have a full understanding of the issues, develop courses of action that could provide a resolution to the problem. There is often more than one way to solve a problem, so it is critical to consider all possible solutions and arrive at several alternatives from which to choose.

Your decision will provide you with an action plan. However, this will be of little value unless it is implemented effectively. Defining how, when, and by whom the action plan is to be implemented and communicating this to those involved is what connects the decision with reality.

Your involvement should not end at implementation, however. Establish criteria for measuring success, then track progress and take corrective actions when necessary. Try to develop and maintain positive attitudes in everyone involved in the implementation process.

IMPLEMENTING
Setting your action plan in motion, by creating a schedule and assigning tasks and responsibilities.

MAKING THE DECISION
Evaluating the alternatives and choosing a course of action that will improve the situation in a significant way.

FOLLOWING THROUGH
Monitoring progress, to ensure that the desired outcome is achieved.

Building power

Power is the capacity to influence an individual or group to behave in ways they would not have on their own. Learning how to acquire power and exercise it effectively will help you manage and influence others and develop your managerial career.

Developing power bases

Managerial positions come with the authority to issue directives and allocate rewards and punishments—for example, to assign favorable or unfavorable work assignments, hold performance reviews, and make salary adjustments. However, you can also build power in other ways:

• Expertise: organizations are often dependent on experts with special skills, such as in technology.

• Charisma: when others admire you and identify with you, you have referent power over them.

• Access to information: having information that only you have access to but others need gives you power.

• Association power: having confidantes in powerful positions can increase your power.

• Impression management: shaping the image you project to others in order to favorably influence how others see and evaluate you can give you power. For example, it might be used when lobbying your boss for a pay raise or a promotion.

• Politicking: you don't always win just by being a competent performer. Politicking is taking actions to influence, or attempt to influence, the distribution of advantages and disadvantages within your organization. It involves using strategies to influence decision outcomes in your favor.

REASONING
Use facts and data to make a logical or rational presentation of ideas. This is most effective when others are trustworthy, open, and logical.

HIGHER AUTHORITY
Gain the support of those above you to back your requests. This is only effective in bureaucratic organizations where there is great respect for authority.

COALITIONS
Develop support in the organization for what you want to happen. This is most effective where final decisions rely on the quantity not the quality of support.

BARGAINING
Exchange benefits or favors to negotiate outcomes acceptable to both parties. This works best when organizational culture promotes give-and-take cooperation.

FRIENDLINESS
Use flattery, create goodwill, act humbly, and be supportive prior to making a request. This works best when you are well liked.

Ways to use managerial power to obtain desired outcomes

SANCTIONS
Use organizationally derived rewards and punishments to obtain desired outcomes. This approach is only for influencing subordinates, and may be seen as manipulative.

ASSERTIVENESS
Be direct and forceful when indicating what you want from others. This strategy is most effective when the balance of power is clearly in your favor.

Managing change

Individuals, managers, teams, and organizations that do not adapt to change in timely ways are unlikely to survive in our increasingly turbulent world environment. Managers that anticipate change, learn to adapt to change, and manage change will be the most successful.

Overcoming resistance

Change is the process of moving from a present state to a more desired state in response to internal and external factors. To successfully implement change, you need to possess the skills to convince others of the need for change, identify gaps between the current situation and desired conditions, and create visions for desirable outcomes.

Experienced managers are aware that efforts to change often face resistance. This can be for a variety of reasons, including fear, vested interests, misunderstanding, lack of trust, differing perceptions of a situation, and limited resources. You need to be able to counter this resistance to change through education, participation, and negotiation.

IN FOCUS... PHASES OF CHANGE

Planned change progresses through three phases:

• **Unfreezing** This involves helping people see that a change is needed because the existing situation is undesirable. Existing attitudes and behaviors need to be altered during this phase to reduce resistance, by explaining how the change can help increase productivity, for example. Your goal in this phase is to help the participants see the need for change and to increase their willingness to make the change a success.

• **Changing** This involves making the actual change and requires you to help participants let go of old ways of doing things and develop new ones.

• **Refreezing** The final phase involves reinforcing the changes made so that the new ways of behaving become stabilized. If people perceive the change to be working in their favor, positive results will serve as reinforcement, but if not, it may be necessary to use external reinforcements, which can be positive or negative.

Promoting change

Major change does not happen easily. Effective managers are able to establish a sense of urgency that the change is needed. If an organization is obviously facing a threat to its survival, this kind of crisis usually gets people's attention. Dramatically declining profits and stock prices are examples. In other cases, when no current crisis is obvious, but managers have identified potential problems by scanning the external environment, the manager needs to find ways to communicate the information broadly and dramatically to make others aware of the need for change. Managers also have to develop and articulate a compelling vision and strategy that people will aspire to, that will guide the change effort. The vision of what it will be like when the change is achieved should illuminate core principles and values that pull followers together. Lastly, institutionalizing changes in the organizational culture will refreeze the change. New values and beliefs will become instilled in the culture so that employees view the changes as normal and integral to the operations of the organization.

TURN TO THE POSITIVE

Try to use any resistance to your proposed change for your benefit, by making it a stimulus for dialog and a deeper, more thoughtful analysis of the alternatives.

Helping others to improve

Helping employees become more competent is an important part of any manager's job. It contributes to a three-way win for the organization, the manager, and the employees themselves. By helping others resolve personal problems and develop skill competencies—and so help them improve their performance—you will motivate your team to achieve better results for themselves and for the organization.

Diagnosing problems

If you can reduce unsatisfactory performance in the people you are managing, you ultimately make your job easier because you will be increasingly able to delegate responsibilities to them. Unsatisfactory performance often has multiple causes. Some causes are within the control of the person experiencing the difficulties, while others are not.

✔ CHECKLIST DETERMINING THE CAUSE OF UNSATISFACTORY PERFORMANCE

	YES	NO
• Is the person unaware that their performance is unsatisfactory? If yes, provide feedback.	☐	☐
• Is the person performing poorly because they are not aware of what is expected of them? If yes, provide clear expectations.	☐	☐
• Is performance hampered by obstacles beyond the person's control? If yes, determine how to remove the obstacles.	☐	☐
• Is the person struggling because they don't know how to perform a key task? If yes, provide coaching or training.	☐	☐
• Is good performance followed by negative consequences? If yes, determine how to eliminate the negative consequences.	☐	☐
• Is poor performance being rewarded by positive consequences? If yes, determine how to eliminate the positive reinforcement.	☐	☐

Ways to help others improve

- Ask questions to help discover sources of problems.
- Accept mistakes and use them as learning opportunities.
- Help develop action plans for improvement.
- Seek to educate rather than to assist.
- Provide meaningful feedback for learning.
- Encourage continual improvement.
- Demonstrate unconditional positive regard by suspending judgement and evaluation.
- Recognize and reward even small improvements.
- Actively listen to employees and show genuine interest.
- Model the behaviors you desire.

Demonstrating positive regard

The relationship between you and the person you are helping is critical to the success of the coaching, mentoring, or counselling you undertake with them. For a helping relationship to be successful it is important to hold the person being helped in "unconditional positive regard". This means that you accept and exhibit warm regard for the person needing help as a person of unconditional self-worth—a person of value no matter what the conditions, problems, or feelings. If you can communicate positive regard, it provides a climate of warmth and safety because the person feels liked and prized as a person. This is a necessary condition for developing the trust that is crucial in a helping relationship.

Conducting a helping session

Before you speak to someone about how to help them improve their performance, make sure you have acquired all the facts about the situation. Take time to think about what type of help the situation requires and consider how the person might react and how they might feel about what you are going to discuss. During the helping session:
• Start by discussing the purpose of the session.
• Try to make the person feel comfortable and at ease.
• Establish a non-defensive climate, characterized by open communication and trust.
• Before you discuss the problem you have identified, raise and discuss positive aspects of the person's performance.
• Mutually define the problem (performance or attitude).
• Mutually determine the causes. Do not interpret or psychoanalyze behavior; instead, ask questions such as, "What's causing the lack of motivation you describe?"
• Help the other person establish an action plan that includes specific goals and dates.
• Make sure expectations are clearly understood.
• Summarize what has been agreed upon.
• Affirm your confidence in the person's ability to make needed changes based on his or her strengths or past history.
   After the session, make sure that you follow up to see how the person is progressing, and modify the action plan if necessary.

 IN FOCUS... FEEDBACK

People need feedback about the consequences of their actions if they are to learn what works and what doesn't and then change their actions to become more effective. Carefully thought-out feedback can increase performance and positive personal development. Applying feedback in the helping process involves:
• Describing observed behaviors and the results and consequences of those behaviors.
• Assessing the impact of the observed behaviors in terms of organizational vision and goals.
• Predicting the personal consequences for the person involved if no changes take place.
• Recommending changes the person could make to improve their behavior.
   This sequence of actions applies whether the type of help being given to the person is coaching, mentoring, or counselling.

Counselling others

Counselling is the discussion of emotional problems in order to resolve them or to help the person better cope. Problems that might require counselling include divorce, serious illness, financial problems, interpersonal conflicts, drug and alcohol abuse, and frustration over a lack of career progress. Although most managers are not qualified as psychologists, there are several things managers can do in a counselling role before referring someone to a professional therapist.

Confidentiality is of paramount importance when counselling others. To open up and share the reasons for many personal problems, people must feel that they can trust you and that there is no threat to their self-esteem or their reputation with others. Emphasize that you will treat in confidence everything that the other person says regarding personal matters.

TIP

BE SUPPORTIVE

Reassure those you are counselling that their problems have solutions and that they have the ability to improve their situation.

Dealing with personal problems

Getting a person to recognize that they have a problem is often the first step in helping them deal with it. You can then follow up by helping them gain insights into their feelings and behaviors, and by exploring the alternatives open to them.

Sometimes people just need a sounding board for releasing tension, which can become a prelude to clarifying the problem, identifying possible solutions, and taking corrective action. Talking things through in a counselling session can help people sort out their feelings into more logical and coherent thoughts.

Above all, be supportive and provide reassurance. People need to know that their problems have solutions. If problems are beyond a person's capability to solve, explain how professional treatment can be obtained, through Employee Assistance Programs, for example, or health plans.

Coaching and mentoring

Coaching is the process of helping people improve performance. A coach analyzes performance, provides insight on how to improve, and offers the leadership, motivation, and supportive climate to help achieve that improvement. In mentoring relationships, a more experienced person formally pairs up with a less experienced one to help show them "the ropes" and to provide emotional support and encouragement.

HOW TO... COACH A PROCESS

Explain and then demonstrate the process.

Observe the person practicing the process.

Provide immediate, specific feedback.

Express confidence in the person's ability.

Agree on follow-up actions.

Helping others develop

As a coach, a manager's job is to help members of their team develop skills and improve. This involves providing instruction, guidance, advice, and encouragement. Effective coaches first establish a supportive climate that promotes development. It is particularly important that you remain non-judgemental and understanding throughout the process, try to solve problems jointly, and educate those you are coaching about how to solve their own problems in the future. As you learn more about the person you are coaching, try to determine the sources of any problems they are having, and provide meaningful feedback.

Mentoring is a broader role. The goal of a mentor is to help a less experienced person achieve his or her career goals. Mentors perform as both coaches and counsellors as they guide their less experienced associates toward improved performance. Mentoring can help new organization members gain a better understanding of the organization's goals, culture, and advancement criteria. It can also help them become more politically savvy and avoid potential career traps. As a mentor, try to help others reduce the stress caused by uncertainty about how to do things and deal with challenging assignments. Be a source of comfort when newer, less experienced people just need to let off steam or discuss career dilemmas.

Three key skills for successful coaching

1
FINDING WAYS TO IMPROVE PERFORMANCE

Help others improve by observing what they do, asking questions, listening, and crafting unique improvement strategies.

3
CREATING A SUPPORTIVE CLIMATE

Use active listening, empower others to implement appropriate ideas, and be available for assistance, guidance, and advice.

2
INFLUENCING OTHERS TO CHANGE THEIR BEHAVIOR

Monitor people's progress and development, and recognize and reward even small improvements.

Be a role model for the qualities that you expect from others, such as openness, commitment, and responsibility.

Involve others in decision-making processes—this helps to encourage people to be responsive to change.

Break large, complex projects into series of simpler tasks—this can boost confidence as the simpler tasks are achieved.

Managing careers

In today's rapidly changing business landscape, managers need to actively manage their careers and provide career guidance to those they are managing. To determine where and how you can best contribute, you need to know yourself, continually develop yourself, and be able to ascertain when and how to change the work you do.

Charting your own career path

Self-assessment is an ongoing process in career management. Successful careers develop when people are prepared for opportunities because they know their strengths, their methods of work, and their values. Self-directed career management is a process by which individuals guide, direct, and influence the course of their careers. This requires exploration and awareness of not only yourself, but also your environment. Individuals who are proactive and collect relevant information about personal needs, values, interests, talents, and lifestyle preferences are more likely to be satisfied and productive when searching for job opportunities, to develop successful career plans, and to be productive in their jobs and careers.

IN FOCUS... CAREER STAGES

Individuals just beginning their careers are usually more concerned with identifying organizations that have the potential to satisfy their career goals and match their values. After settling into a job, focus shifts to achieving initial successes, gaining credibility, learning to get along with their boss, and managing image.

Managers in the middle of their careers are more concerned with career reappraisal, overcoming obsolescence owing to technological advances, and becoming more of a generalist. In the later stages of their careers, managers focus more on teaching others and leaving a contribution before retirement.

Driving forward

The first step in self-directed career management is planning. Taking your strengths, limitations, and values into account, start searching the environment for matching opportunities. Use the information you gather to establish realistic career goals and then develop a strategy to achieve them. As you progress through your career plan, regularly undertake performance appraisals to make sure that you are remaining on track and that your goals haven't changed.

Directing others

The most important thing you can do to contribute to the career development of others is to instill in them the need to take responsibility for managing their own careers. Then you can provide support that will enable those you are managing to add to their skills, abilities, and knowledge, in order to maintain their employability within the organization. To help those you are managing develop their careers:

• Keep your team updated about the organization's goals and future strategies so that they will know where the organization is headed and be better able to develop a personal career development plan to share in that future.

• Create growth opportunities for your team, to give them new, interesting, and professionally challenging work experiences.

• Offer financial assistance, such as tuition reimbursement for college courses or skills training.

• Allow paid time off from work for off-the-job training, and ensure that those you are managing have reasonable workloads so that they are not precluded from having time to develop new skills, abilities, and knowledge.

Index

Acknowledgments

Author's acknowledgments

This book would not have been created without the initiation, guidance, perseverance, and flexibility of Kati Dye at cobalt id. We also want to thank Peter Jones at Dorling Kindersley for his assistance and adaptability in managing the schedule and business side of this project.

Publisher's acknowledgments

The publisher would like to thank Hilary Bird for indexing, Judy Barratt for proofreading, and Chuck Wills for coordinating Americanization.